First hardcover edition June 2019

Written by Megan Gillett

Illustrations & book design by Cloé Auneau

ISBN 978-1-9161-4290-9 (hardcover)

Dear Little Person,

Here is a book especially for you, it is a special book to help you be happy and worry less. It is yours to share with family, friends, teachers, neighbours, coaches, strangers, even next-door's grumpy cat. In fact, here is a book for you to share with everyone, because happiness is the loveliest of gifts to share, even better than sharing the last slice of chocolate cake.

Grown-ups can think that being a child is easy and that you are always happy but sometimes you aren't and that is A-okay. It is normal to feel sad or angry or frustrated or like you want to scream so loud that you'll wake the tiny little mice with the tiny little ears at the bottom of the garden. Our emotions make us who we are but they can also make us feel things we don't want to, or act ways we don't understand. We are here to help you learn about all of those feelings from the good ones to the bad ones and to explore all the ways we can make your heart shine that little bit brighter.

We want you to be happy because feeling happy is the greatest, most wonderful, joyful, super-duper trooper, put on your wellies and dance in the rain feeling the world has to offer. Happiness my gorgeous, little person is what you deserve so get cosy, get your thinking cap on and let's go on a journey to find it.

Megan

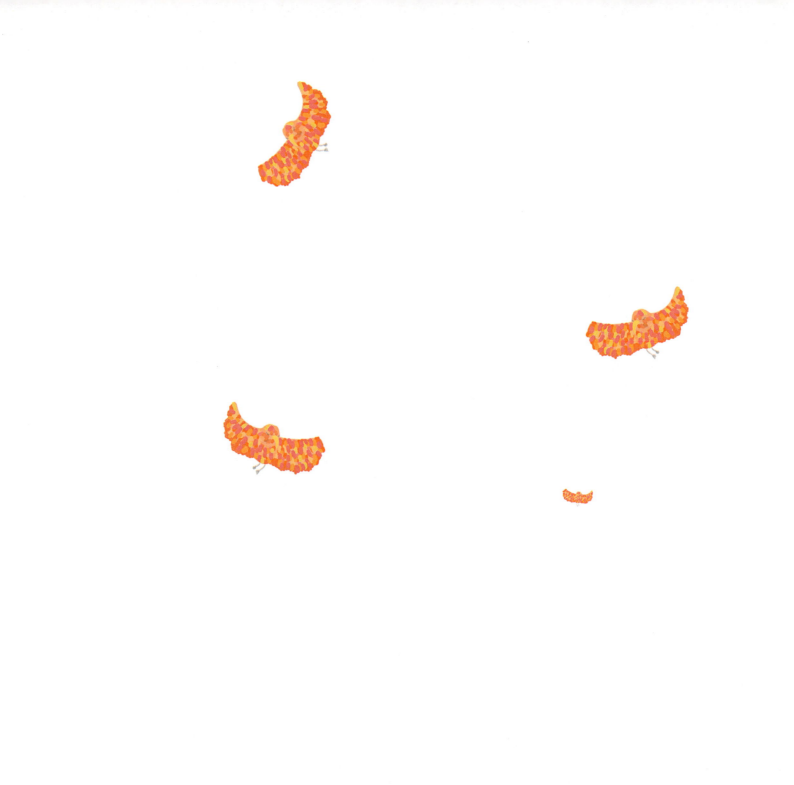

Contents

Identifying Emotions

Often my head feels full of words and my heart feels full of feelings but my mouth can't speak them,

This is because sometimes we don't know what we are feeling or how to express it, even grown-ups can struggle to say how they are feeling and when this happens we need a little extra help to work it out.

Feelings and emotions are what make us human, we can feel lots of emotions at the same time or we can feel one emotion more often than any other emotion. Working out how we are feeling can help us to explain to others why we are acting like we are.

Have a look at the emotions below.

I feel proud when the teacher praises me at school

I feel scared when my Mummy shouts at me louder than she normally does

I feel excited when it is my birthday

I feel angry when my brother or sister breaks my toy

I feel disappointed when my Daddy says he will play with me but is then too busy

1

When we have feelings or emotions it can make us do things we wouldn't normally do. If we are angry we might shout or hurt someone, if we are sad we might cry. If we are excited we might jump up and down, if we are shy we might be quieter than usual and if we are confused we might be naughty because we don't want anyone to know we don't understand. Talking about our feelings and emotions may be hard but it helps us grow up happy and we all want to be happy.

Take the time now to sit down with your Mum or Dad to talk about what feelings you feel the most and how you act when you have these feelings

I feel happy when I go swimming with my family

I feel sad when my friends leave me out

I feel embarrassed when someone teases me in front of my friends

I feel confused when someone asks me a question and I don't know the answer

I feel shy when I meet new people

What makes you happy?

Being happy makes us feel like the sun is shining on us even when it is raining or like hundreds of butterflies are tickling our skin with their wings or like being cuddled up warm and safe in the fur of a snuggly polar bear.

This is because being happy is the most special of feelings.

Sometimes you might feel like things stop you from being happy. School, friends or family might make you feel sad, or you might get scared or worried and this means you find it harder to jump on the happy train and hoot the horn of happiness (feel free to loudly hoot the horn of happiness right now).

If this happens then you need to talk to Mummy or Daddy about why you're not feeling happy because when we share our worries they quite often disappear.

3

If you are just feeling a little blue and don't know how to shake it off or you are feeling worried and can't stop thinking of your worries then it can be helpful to have a happy pack. To get your happy pack ready you need to think of what makes you feel the happiest.

Here are some examples of what makes us happy:

I feel happy when my Mummy gives me a big, squishy cuddle
I feel happy and calm when I lie on my back and watch the clouds floating above me
I feel happy when I watch my favourite film
I feel happy when I play dress up
I feel happy when I play with my best friend
I feel happy when I am running in the park
I feel happy when I am by myself colouring in

Now think of ten things that make you feel happy and get them written or drawn down in a book so that when you next feel a little sad or are worrying you can go to your happy pack and do one of the things on your list to make yourself feel better.

Happy place

People can be mean and when they are this can make you feel sad or sometimes you can just have a really bad day that leaves you feeling unhappy. If you feel like this, there is a place you can go where your sadness isn't allowed to follow, where only your happy head can go. This place is called your happy place.

A happy place is a magical land you travel to in your mind where you can imagine all of your favourite things; all of your favourite people and a place that makes you feel calm just as soon as you think of it.

I like to go to my happy place when my head is jumbled with thoughts or when I am bored in the car or when I feel a little bit lonely. It helps me to feel that whatever is happening or wherever I am, there is always a place I can go where no one else can follow and where I am completely safe.

Now let me tell you all about my happy place and how I get there, lets go there together

I close my eyes and I see myself lying on a sandy beach in a polka dot swimsuit, the sand is white and the sea is a beautiful blue. I imagine myself feeling the sand between my fingers and I imagine the sound of the waves meeting the shore.

I can feel the warmth of the sun on my skin as I push my toes into the warm sand and breathe deeply smelling the salty air of the beach. There are pigs swimming in the sea that 'oink' a hello at me and brightly coloured parrots that squawk from the palm trees as I feel all my worries disappearing from my body.

No sadness or anger or worry or fear is allowed in my happy place, at my special beach, only happy thoughts are allowed here.

Why don't you draw a picture of what your happy place looks like? Is it playing football in the park? Or snuggling up with Mummy surrounded by your favourite teddies? Or is it dancing with your friends to your favourite band?

Try and imagine your happy place, how it sounds, how it smells, what you can see and most importantly how it makes you feel. Whenever you feel sadness creeping in your head go to your happy place and remember all these things to help you push the sadness out.

6

Worry

Worry is a feeling we get when we think about something and it makes us feel not quite right, as if we are scared or nervous. We may worry when we think about doing something or when we meet someone new or if we hear about something happening to someone else as it may then make us think about what if it happened to us. It is normal to worry and worrying can be helpful as it helps us to work out things we didn't realise we were scared of or things we didn't realise we needed to talk about.

Worry isn't a very nice feeling and it can make us act differently to how we normally would. It can feel like a drum in your chest or make you struggle to sleep. It might make you feel like crying or like you don't want to do something. It can make you lash out in anger because you don't know how to say what is worrying you or it may even make you wet the bed. The worry you are feeling can be quite hard to find because of this, it can hide deep inside making you feel bad and so we have to work out what it is by talking about it out so that we can get you back to your happy place.

Worry can pop up at any time and different things can make it say hello, going to school may make you worried because your friends may leave you out or be mean or you may find your school work hard. You may feel worried when you are in new situations or meet new people or you may worry about something bad happening. This is all very normal and we have to remember worry is different for everyone, what your Mummy worries about will probably be very different to what your best friend worries about.

The first thing to do to get rid of worry is working out why it has come to visit and then just like a grumpy old relative who acts like a mood Hoover, sucking up all your happiness whenever they come to your home, we need to find a way to get rid of it.

My favourite way of saying goodbye to worry is using a worry jar

Now the worry jar is there for everyone in the family, as everyone will have worry visit them at some point. The worry jar or the magical pot of captured worries as I like to call it, is something for the whole family to use. Here are the steps on how to make your worry jar and how to make it magic.

Worry jar

Step One: (This is the easiest) Get a jar or a pot or a box

Step Two: Decorate it however you want

Step Three: Put it somewhere in your home that is easy for everyone to reach, ready for when you have a worry

Step Four: When you feel a worry, write it down on a piece of paper or get Mummy or Daddy to do it for you

Step Five: Fold up the piece of paper and put it in the jar but when you do, you have to say these magic words 'Worry I see you and I'm saying hello but now it is time for you to go'

Step Six: Wait till the next day and it will have magically disappeared from the jar. The thing about worry is, by realising what is bothering you and talking about it you can often make it go away. Remember with worry you have the power to make it disappear just like a rubber on your drawing when you have made a mistake

Kindness

Being kind means treating others how you would like to be treated yourself. It is acting with love and thinking of ways to make other people happy. If everyone was kinder to each other then the world would see more smiles and it is our job as humans to help make the world happier, from the ocean to the orang-utans to the people. You can help do this by being kind to a person or to the planet or to an animal and if you can make someone smile, even a stranger by being kind then you are already helping. Remember smiles make the world go around that little bit easier.

Showing kindness to others doesn't have to be difficult, in fact it can be easy and if we all did small acts of kindness when we could it would build one gigantic act of kindness and kindness glitter would rain from the clouds. Kindness is the one gift we can give that doesn't cost any money and it is often the easiest kind of gift to give, so get out there and gift the world your kindness.

Here are some ideas for the little things you can do to help make the world a better place:

Buying a homeless person some food

Pick up plastic on the beach

Paint a picture or message on a stone and leave it somewhere that someone else will find it

Make a member of your family's bed for them or make all your family members beds

Feed lettuce to the ducks in the park

Donate all your old toys and clothes to charity

Hold the door open for the person behind you

Tell someone they are special to you

Draw a picture for your elderly neighbour

Bake your teacher a cake as a thank you for helping you learn

Tell a joke to someone who looks sad

Can you think of anything else you could do that would show kindness? Pick a day this week when you could show extra kindness and then a day for every week that follows and when we act with kindness it in turn helps us to be happy

Gratefulness

In life we need tools to fix things, a doctor has their stethoscope, a mechanic has their wrench, an artist has their paint brush and a happy person has their secret weapon, their special tool, that always helps them look on the sunny side of life, do you know what it is? Can you guess?

It is ... gratefulness! This means thinking about all the magical, amazing, special things we do have rather than all the things we don't have. For example, I don't have a jungle tree house with a swimming pool and a machine that provides an endless supply of ice cream but I do have a lovely home with a big, slobbery dog named Wilma.

We have to remember and appreciate all the things we do have because there may be other people who have so much less, they may not have a home or food to eat or a family, If we focus or what we do have then we think about what we don't have a lot less.

Happy, optimistic people practice saying thank you for what they are grateful for and I know you want to be a happy, optimistic person otherwise you wouldn't be reading this book so lets have a think now about what makes you lucky.

Is it your loving family? Your warm home? Your favourite toy? The food in your tummy? Your Granny? Being able to run around on the grass?

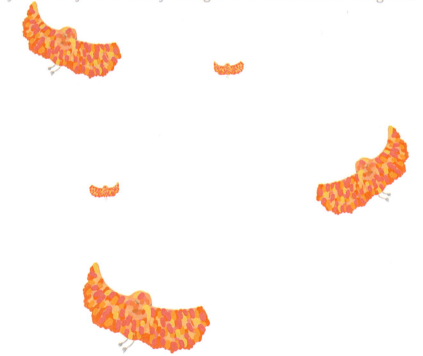

Talk about this now with your family, all say something that makes you feel lucky. If you do this every day and make it part of your routine or part of your good habits then it will help you to carry happiness in your heart always

Gifts and talents

Different people are good at different things, if we were all good at the same things then the world would be a very boring place, our differences mean we all come with special gifts and these gifts fill the world with all the colours of the rainbow. We must not get sad or frustrated when others are better than us at doing things because for them that is when their rainbow gift is shining, another time may come when they are not as good as us at something and we shine instead. That is the beauty of being a human being, we are all unique and we all shine differently.

It is great for us to celebrate what we are good at because it helps us to still feel proud of ourselves when we do things we aren't so good at but it also helps us to do one very important thing, it helps us to love ourselves. Loving ourselves is very important if we want to be happy because if we are mean to ourselves and tell ourselves off for not being good at things then we will only make ourselves feel sad. You need to be your own cheerleader, you need to learn how to cheer yourself on when you are good or bad at things because this is how you stay happy.

13

Here is me being my own cheer leader by listing some things I am good at:

Using my imagination to create stories

Being kind to my brother

Making my friend's laugh when I tell jokes

Dancing

Building creations with Lego

Being kind and looking after animals

Reading

What are you good at? Don't be shy be proud of your rainbow gifts because they are yours and yours alone. Make sure to ask your family what their gifts and talents are and if they can't think of any, remind them why they are so special.

Habits

Habits are part of everyday life, we all have different habits, some are good and some are bad. Bad habits could be picking your nose and eating it or throwing your litter on the floor rather than putting it in the bin. We try to train ourselves (or our parents do) to break or stop bad habits because they are often not very nice for other people to see or live with.

When we want to start good habits, we must train our brains by doing things over and over until we do them without thinking. A good habit can be cleaning our teeth before bed or eating the yukky broccoli on our dinner plate but it can also be learning to have special skills in place to keep us feeling happy or calm.

If I feel a bad feeling then I do a few things to make my mind feel happier or more relaxed. I go for a walk or I watch my favourite film or I dance to my happy song or I cuddle my dog or I kick a ball. I make sure every time I think of a worry or something that makes me feel sad, frustrated or angry I do a good habit like listening to a happy or calming song rather than a bad habit like having a temper tantrum.

Have a think about how feeling sad, worried, frustrated or angry might make you act and now think of how you could use a special tool from your happy pack to turn your bad habit into a good one. It could even be as easy as training yourself to say 'I am feeling really angry and I don't know why' rather than shouting or hurting someone.

Here are some more happy pack ideas that your family could help you with if you are acting out your bad habits more often than your good ones. Add more ideas to your happy pack for all the negative feelings on the feelings page by thinking of something that would help you to feel better for each of the ones that make you feel bad.

Extra happy pack ideas

Ask for a cuddle whenever you need it and have family cuddle time, a time where your whole family snuggle together

Create a special sentence or phrase with your family that is your family's secret mantra. You can say it to each other when one of you is feeling down or upset, as it will help you to feel calm and an important member of your family

Create a special action like a secret handshake or a way to be affectionate that just you and your family know about, use it in the same way as the phrase

Play a calming or fun song to pull you out of your feeling, use the same one every time so that your brain recognises it and knows to relax

Do some crafts or a sport or even stand on the spot and do star jumps, this will trick your brain, it will be so busy concentrating on whatever you are doing that it will forget how you were feeling

This page might feel quite hard to do or confusing and it might feel like it takes a long time to turn your bad habits into good ones.

A lot of adults still can't do this, but, once you've got it, it's a skill you will have for the rest of your life so keep at it happiness warriors because if you start now by the time you are all grown up you will be a master at creating good habits.

Meditation and Relaxation

One of the best skills you can have in your happy pack is meditation. Meditation is a way to make your mind feel like an empty room, without worries or thoughts making it all messy. It can help to make you feel relaxed and calm when you feel all jumbled with thoughts. Meditation is a beautiful tool for happiness but it can take a lot of practice and concentration in the beginning, so don't be hard on yourself if you struggle to get it straight away.

First you need to find a spot in your house that is both comfy and quiet and then you need to sit down with your legs crossed (don't lie down as it is easy to fall asleep).

Now set a timer for just a couple of minutes, the more you practice the more minutes you can add on but for now just try for two.

Shall we give it a go?

Here comes the difficult part, clearing your mind of all the chaos and making it feel like a swimming pool before anyone gets in. The best way to achieve this is to breathe, something we all do without thinking but now you must think about it, the deeper you breathe the more your head will clear.

A helpful way to do this is to imagine there are balloons in front of your face and when you gently breathe out you blow the balloons further away from you. Lets try it, breathe deeply in through your nose for a count of four seconds and then breathe slowly out of your mouth for a count of six seconds imagining those colourful balloons blowing further and further away.

Thoughts may come in to your head and that is okay but every time they do try and go back to thinking of the balloons. Repeat the breathing in and out for the full two minutes and feel the calm wash over you.

There are a couple of other things you can do to make it easier, one of them is having a special trinket, pillow or ornament to have with you during it that makes you feel calm and the other is to play relaxing music in the background.

That, little happiness warriors, is meditation. It can be very hard to clear the mind of all your thoughts but mediation can help you achieve happiness until you are grey and old.

Affirmation Cards

We all need reminders that we are wonderful and whatever our age it can sometimes be easy to forget. These cards are here to help you understand how special and loved you truly are, so when you need a little extra help to remember this get them out and either read them if you can or get someone else to read them to you and then repeat the message back.

Say the sentences loud and proud.

If you don't like these cards you can make your own but only if they are filled with positive words.

19

Affirmation cards

21

I am the most loved **child in the world**

I am kind

I am a good friend

I am beautiful
even when I make mistakes

I am an important
member of my family

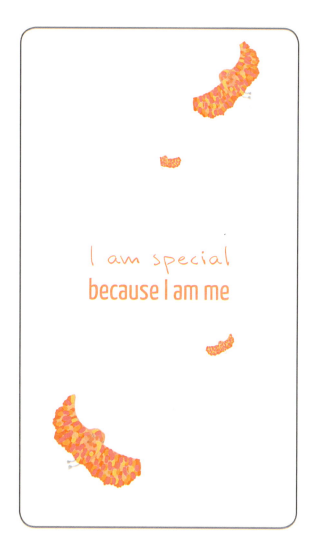

I am special
because I am me

25

I am smart

I am full of great
ideas.

I am fun
to be around.

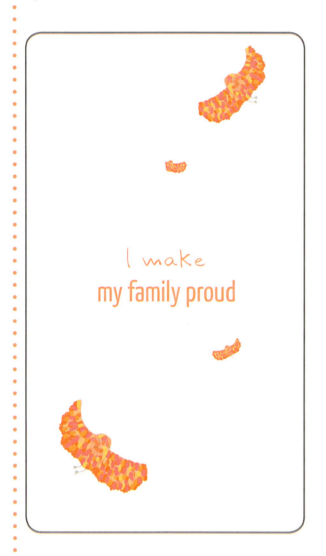

I make
my family proud

Lightning Source UK Ltd.
Milton Keynes UK
UKRC021114300819
348899UK00001B/1